Costume in Context

The Edwardians

and the First World War

Jennifer Ruby

B.T. Batsford Ltd, London

Foreword

When studying costume it is important to understand the difference between fashion and costume. Fashion tends to predict the future – that is, what people *will* be wearing – and very fashionable clothes are usually worn only by people wealthy enough to afford them. For example, even today, the clothes that appear in fashionable magazines are not the same as those being worn by the majority of people in the street. Costume, on the other hand, represents what people are actually wearing at a given time, which may be quite different from what is termed 'fashionable' for their day.

Each book in this series is built round a fictitious family. By following the various members, sometimes over several generations – and the people with whom they come into contact – you will be able to see the major fashion developments of the period and compare the clothing and lifestyles of people from all walks of life. You will meet servants, soldiers, street-sellers and beggars as well as the very wealthy, and you will see how their different clothing reflects their particular occupations and circumstances.

Major social changes are mentioned in each period and you will see how clothing is adapted as people's needs and attitudes change. The date list will help you to understand more fully how historical events affect the clothes that people wear.

Many of the drawings in these books have been taken from contemporary paintings. During the course of your work perhaps you could visit some museums and art galleries yourself in order to learn more about the costumes of the period you are studying from the artists who painted at that time.

Acknowledgments

300490174

The sources for the colour illustrations in this book have, in some cases, been paintings and contemporary fashion plates. In particular: 'Laundry Girls', after Albert Rutherston; 'In the garden' after an advertisement for His Master's Voice, c. 1909; 'Dress for a garden party'; After J. Gose; 'Dress for the races' from *Journal des Dames et des Modes*, 1913; 'Afternoon dress' from *Luxe de Paris*, 1913; 'The tango' and 'Lady in pink' from *Journal des Dames et des Modes*, 1914.

The extract on page 16 is from Noel Streatfield (ed.), *The Day Before Yesterday*, Collins, 1956. The list on page 53 is from W.A.A.C. Headquarters, Circular 37. Wom. Coll. Amy 3.13.

My grateful thanks also to Joan Lock for kindly providing me with information on the uniform of the women police.

© Jennifer Ruby 1988
First published 1988
Reprinted 1994

Typeset by Tek-Art Ltd, Kent
and printed in Great Britain by
The Bath Press, Avon
for the publishers
B.T. Batsford Ltd
4 Fitzhardinge Street
London W1H 0AH

ISBN 0 7134 5605 1

Contents

Date List

1901	King Edward VII comes to the throne.
1903	The first motor taxi comes to London. The Women's Social and Political Union is formed in Manchester. The headquarters are transferred to London in 1905.
1904	The first motor bus in London.
1906	The Trade Disputes Act allows for 'peaceful picketing' and collective bargaining on the part of the trade unions.
1908	The Wright brothers fly in public for the first time.
1909	Old age pensions are introduced. The Trade Board Act fixes a legal minimum wage for factory workers.
1910	Death of King Edward. Succeeded by his son George V. The V.A.D. organization comes into existence.
1911	National Insurance is introduced. By paying a small weekly sum people can register with a doctor and obtain free medical treatment. They can also insure against loss of wages during sickness and unemployment. The Russian Ballet Company comes to London.
1913	The Suffragette Emily Wilding Davison throws herself under the King's horse on Derby day.
1914	War is declared. Thousands of women rush to join the V.A.D.s. The Women Police Volunteers is started by Nina Boyle and led by Miss Damer Dawson.
1915	The Women's Police Service is started by Miss Damer Dawson.
1916	The Women's Auxiliary Army Corps and the Women's Land Army are founded.
1918	The war ends. Women over 30 with some property, and all men over 21, are given the vote. Unemployment insurance is made universal and the 'dole' is introduced.

Introduction

The period covered by this book (1901-18), is only a short one, yet these few years saw some of the greatest social upheavals the world has ever known. Many changes took place which greatly affected lifestyles, attitudes and styles of dress.

The Edwardian Era (1901-10) was one of extravagant luxury. It was the last time that the court would dictate the fashions, and King Edward and his beautiful Queen Alexandra seemed to set an example of elegant splendour. Ladies corsetted themselves into beautiful and elaborate dresses of silk and crepe with long trains and an abundance of fancy trimmings, while the men were stiffly formal in their morning coats and frock coats and silk top hats. For the rich, life revolved around country house parties and the 'Season' in London. They were constantly dressing and undressing, each occasion demanding a different outfit, whether for walking, riding, shooting, dancing, dining, motoring or any of the other pursuits that they enjoyed. In fact, they worked very hard at having a good time.

At the other end of the social scale were the poor, many of whom lived in slums and worked hard for low wages. Large numbers of women were employed in the 'sweated trades', making items such as sacks, matchboxes and toothbrushes, or sewing the fine garments worn by the rich, in order to earn a little extra money for their families. Men and women worked in the factories for long hours in terrible conditions and received low wages in return. Some people began to feel resentment, believing that they were starving to death in a land of plenty. Because of this, the trade union movement, aimed as it was at improving conditions for working people, grew rapidly in popularity. However, those with jobs were the lucky ones. Unemployment was high and the constant threat of the workhouse was a fear lurking in the background for many.

In between these two extremities were the middle classes. Professional people like doctors, lawyers and solicitors and self-made men, who made their wealth from trade and industry. On the whole, these people were comfortably off. They tended to live in large houses and had servants to look after them.

In 1909 things began to change. The new Liberal government introduced old-age pensions, and this meant that for the first time the state would give a regular income to people over 70. The allowance was not enough to live on, but if it were supplemented with savings and help from their children it enabled old people to retire and keep their dignity and self-respect. In the same year, the first Trade Board Act fixed a legal minimum wage for factory workers, and over the next few years a national system of labour exchanges was set up. These were designed to help the unemployed find work and also to pay them unemployment benefit whilst they were looking for jobs. These changes were the beginning of what we now know as the welfare state.

In 1910 King Edward died and was succeeded by his son George V. This event did not in itself have any great effect on the fashion scene, but there were changes taking place at this time. Paul Poiret, a famous fashion designer, was beginning to make his influence felt. He had a marvellous sense of colour and began introducing striking, strong colours into his designs, in place of the soft mauves, pinks and blues that had been popular. He also favoured soft drapery as opposed to

The sporting life, c. 1903

motoring outfit

wool golfing costume

flannel boating suit

wool cycling costume with leather lapels, cuffs, pocket flaps and buttons

cotton swimming costume

the rigid, corsetted garments that ladies had been wearing. Some of his ideas had been inspired by the Russian ballet, which was touring Europe at this time, and the new fashions were taken up enthusiastically by many women. Skirts became very narrow. The hobble skirt was extremely popular and prevented women walking with anything other than short shuffling steps. It is very interesting that fashion was dictating the wearing of these restricting skirts at the very time that the Suffragettes were campaigning for more freedom for women!

There were, therefore, rumblings of change afoot on both the social scene and the fashion front before war broke out in 1914. However, when the war did begin it accelerated these changes and altered the lifestyles and attitudes of many people.

The war brought the fashion market to a virtual standstill. Materials were in short supply and, in any case, soldiers had to be provided for before materials could be used for fashionable clothes. Also, many women began to work in men's jobs and therefore the demand was for more practical garments made from practical fabrics. The men returning home on leave from the front must have been surprised at the changes. They had left their womenfolk behind in restricting hobble skirts and returned to find many of them in overalls and trousers!

Men from all classes fought side by side in the war and women proved themselves equal to men by doing men's jobs. There followed, therefore, a relaxing of social conventions as people from all walks of life and from both sexes worked together. This, of course, had to result in a change in attitudes, and after the war things could never revert back to how they had been at the beginning of the century. It was no longer taken for granted that everyone had a particular place in society and that some must be more privileged than others. After all, if people were thought to be equal when it came to fighting for their country they ought also to be equal when it came to privileges. It seemed as if some of the old rigid class and sex divisions were beginning to dissolve. Working-class people began to stand up for their rights and women over 30 were given the vote. This was still a long way from the society that we know today but it was a great step forward.

All these changes were reflected in the clothes that people wore. In general, dress became less formal and more practical. It was as if there had been a kind of relaxing of the rules governing dress as well as the rules governing society. Also, more clothes were being mass produced, which made them cheaper and available to more people.

Fashion always reflects the age. Think carefully about some of the points mentioned above as you follow the characters through this book and see if you can trace the relationship between changes on the social scene and changes in dress.

A Rich Landowner, c. 1903

This is Lord Dudley who lives in a large country mansion in Dorset. He owns a great deal of land and is very rich, so he can afford to buy fashionable, good-quality clothes for himself and his family.

Here you can see him wearing a morning coat with a matching waistcoat and striped trousers. The morning coat is easily recognizable by its fronts, which are cut sloping from the waist. This was a popular coat and could be worn on its own or as a suit with matching waistcoat and trousers. Lord Dudley's coat and waistcoat are black, and his cashmere trousers are light grey with a dark grey stripe. Over his shoes he is wearing white spats made of drill cloth and he is carrying his gloves and cane.

On the opposite page you can see him dressed in a more informal outfit, which he might wear whilst out walking or shooting in the country. It consists of a straw boater, tweed morning coat and waistcoat, breeches, leather gaiters and stout shoes.

Also pictured opposite are a few other items from Lord Dudley's wardrobe. The hats and canes are part of a large collection which he possesses.

lightweight bowler

golf hat

tweed hat

deerstalker

silk top hat

patent dress shoe

tennis shoe

canvas waistcoat embroidered with cotton and panels of silk

spats — elastic under shoe arch

boots

silver

ivory

'Oxford' stick holding ten cigarettes and a match-box!

silver stick used as pipe-holder

walking sticks

The Landowner's Wife, c. 1903

Here is Lady Constance Dudley. She is wearing a light muslin day dress trimmed with ribbon and lace, a straw hat decorated with flowers, and she is carrying a dainty parasol.

The bodice and skirt of her dress are, in fact, two separate garments made to match, and underneath them she is wearing her petticoats and corset. At this time it was fashionable for ladies to wear corsets, like the one pictured opposite, which accentuated the bust and bottom but flattened the stomach. This look was called the 'S-bend' shape.

You can also see here other items from Lady Constance's wardrobe. Two interesting articles are the button hooks and dress clips. Button hooks were used to help prevent a fashionable lady from having to stoop too much whilst doing up the long row of buttons on her boots. Dress clips were worn suspended from the waist on a tiny cord and were used to lift the skirt from dirty pathways.

Lady Constance's garments may look very beautiful, but they were difficult to clean without today's sophisticated washing and dry cleaning methods. It was the job of a lady's maid to care for her mistress's clothes. She would use petrol to remove some of the stains. This left the clothes with a strong odour, so they had to be hung outside to air. Sometimes a maid would use a mixture of fuller's earth, ammonia and benzine. Any material that was unwashable – for example, white silk – was cleaned with stale breadcrumbs.

Compare the time taken to care for Lady Constance's garments with the time it takes for us to clean our clothes today.

hat decorated with flowers and ostrich plumes

morning cap

lace collar

corset giving the 'S-bend' shape

blouse

shoes

kid boots

scalloped edge

button hooks

rubber boots and galoshes

spring inside

dress clips

The Landowner's Children, c. 1905

Here is Lord Dudley's eldest daughter, Elizabeth, who is 15.

She is wearing a dainty dress of cotton voile with blue spots. Once again, the dress has a separate bodice and skirt, both of which are decorated with frills and flounces. The bodice belt is made of blue taffeta and her parasol is of chiffon.

Two of her brothers, Alfred and William, are pictured opposite. They are aged 11 and 12 and are dressed in smart grey suits with patterned ties. Both boys have watch chains. Their clothes seem very stiff and formal compared to those worn by boys of a similar age today.

Although these children come from a wealthy family and have servants to wait on them, their strictly disciplined lives are not easy. They are expected to dress correctly and behave politely at all times.

The boys are required to work hard at their private school in order to become well educated, and Elizabeth must work hard at becoming a 'lady'. Part of her education will be in the art of entertaining. For example, she must learn that at afternoon tea a lady never pours the milk into the cup before the tea and she must remember not to remove her gloves when taking tea at other people's houses. There is no question of her being able to choose a career or become independent in any way. If Elizabeth could see into the future do you think she would wish to swap her cushioned and chaperoned existence for the freedom of today's women?

The Younger Children, c. 1905

This is Amy, who is five years old. She is wearing a pleated dress decorated with lace and ribbons, and she has ribbons in her hair. Amy's clothes are far more restricting than those worn by today's five-year-olds, and she is hampered by many underclothes, some of which are pictured below. In the winter she wears a vest, a bodice, drawers, a flannel petticoat and a cotton petticoat under her dress. In the summer the flannel petticoat is exchanged for a cotton one. Young children also wore gaiters in the winter. These were usually fur lined and had elastic under the foot. You can see Amy's in the picture below.

In the nursery, opposite, are Alex, who is six, and three-year-old James. Alex is wearing a sailor suit, which was a popular outfit for little boys. As it was the custom to dress boys as girls until the age of five, James is still encumbered by a dress. It has an abundance of frills, flounces and embroidery.

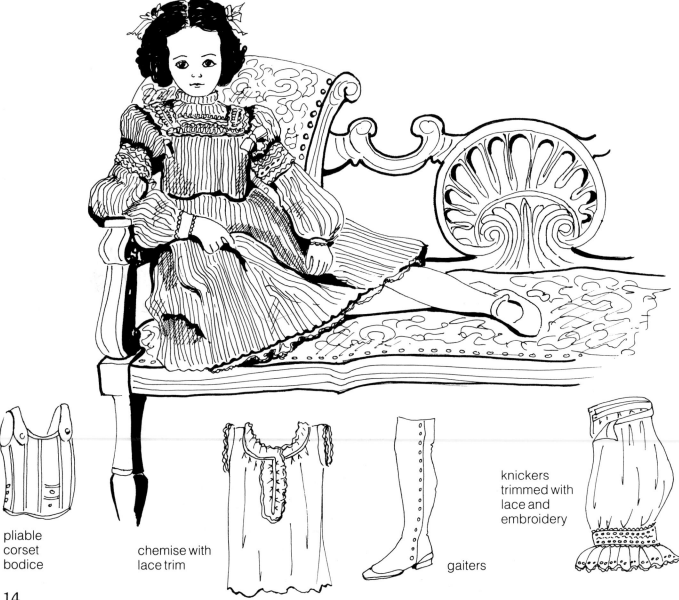

pliable
corset
bodice

chemise with
lace trim

gaiters

knickers
trimmed with
lace and
embroidery

Young Edwardian children had to put up with a lot of dressing up and they wore many more layers of clothing than children do today. No matter how hot it might be, winter clothes were worn until May was out, and summer clothes, whatever the weather, until the end of September. Like their older brothers and sister, Alex and James also lead disciplined lives, with their meals as regular as clockwork, two walks a day, an hour with their parents in the evening (for which they must dress up), and a story from their nurse before bedtime.

How does this compare with the lifestyle of children of a similar age today? How have our attitudes towards children's clothes changed, do you think?

The Children's Nurse, c. 1905

This is the children's nanny, Edith. She is sitting with five-year-old Jonathan on her knee. As it is morning, she is wearing a long, cotton print dress, a white apron with the bib pinned to her dress, and a small cap and brooch. In the afternoons she changes into a smart black dress.

Edith has been with the family for many years. She comes from a poor background and started her working life as a maid waiting on the nursery. She then became under-nurse and, finally, was promoted to head nurse. The children love her because they are so familiar with her. She spends much more time with them than their own parents do. Lord and Lady Dudley only see their younger children once a day when they are allowed downstairs.

The life of a children's nurse was not an easy one, as one nurse wrote:

'It was the way the children had to be turned out that made so much work. Although there was a laundress for large things, we did all the small washing, and the nappies, and of course all the children's mending. The clothes to be worn the next morning were always pressed overnight, but it was ribbons that took the most time. In those days drawers had ribbons run through them, and little bows sewn on them. Petticoats had ribbons round the neck, sleeves and bottom, and all those ribbons had to be pressed before they were threaded.'

Two Parlourmaids, c. 1905

Susan and Ellen are parlourmaids at the mansion. In the mornings they wear cotton print dresses for cleaning, but in the afternoons they change into smart black dresses, starched aprons and small white caps. This is because they might be required to serve tea for their mistress.

The collars and cuffs of the girls' dresses are detachable and have to be washed and starched regularly so that they are always crisp and clean.

A Country Doctor and His Wife, c. 1905

Robert Westlake is the local village doctor. He is quite comfortably off but not, of course, as wealthy as Lord Dudley. Dr Westlake is an important part of the village community, and as he is the only doctor in the village he knows all the residents personally.

The doctor has a car, the only one in the village apart from Lord Dudley's, so he strikes an imposing figure when he visits his patients.

The doctor is wearing a silk top hat (in which he keeps his stethoscope), a frock coat, a double-breasted waistcoat and light-coloured wool trousers. His frock coat is a little old fashioned, but Robert Westlake is an older man than Lord Dudley and is not as up-to-date with his clothing.

Many of the illnesses in Edwardian times were different to those of today. Typhoid, diphtheria and whooping cough were common, and people often died from pneumonia. Villagers would not call in a doctor unless there was a real emergency, however. Many women had as many as ten children and, therefore, knew a good deal about illness and frequently helped each other.

The doctor's wife, Mrs Westlake, is always smart and wears good-quality clothes but, of course, she does not have an extensive wardrobe like Constance Dudley.

Here she is wearing a silk afternoon dress trimmed with lace and cord tassels. The bodice and skirt are separate, and the skirt is lined with cotton.

Like her husband, Mrs Westlake is a respected figure in the village, and she often helps the needy by taking them small food parcels.

The Doctor's Children, c. 1905

This is the doctor's daughter, Anne. She is wearing a high-necked blouse with a lace yoke, and a skirt which is made of light wool. Over her blouse she has a fitted jacket of navy serge.

Anne has learned to type and often helps in her father's surgery. Her clothes need to be practical, so she tends to wear blouses and skirts, or tailor-made costumes, rather than frilly dresses. Also, Anne does not have the large clothes allowance that Elizabeth has.

Anne is hoping eventually to work in London, as her brother has told her that it would be possible for her to get a good position as a private secretary there. She could probably work for an M.P. or a solicitor and live in their house. Her parents are not happy about the idea, but Anne is a strong-willed girl and will probably have her way.

Opposite you can see Richard Westlake, who is visiting his parents. He usually lives in London, where he is studying at St Bartholemew's hospital to become a doctor.

Richard is wearing a tweed lounge coat which has a pleat and a short belt at the back. His flannel trousers are quite narrow in the leg and have turn-ups. He is also wearing a waistcoat, a very stiff collar and a striped tie.

When Richard is at the London hospital, he wears a doctor's coat like the one pictured here. It is made of washable cotton drill but is beige rather than white because he is a student and not a fully qualified doctor.

Sometimes he helps with operations. When he does he wears a surgeon's operating coat. It is made of holland and the back is open to allow for ventilation.

It is interesting that rubber gloves, which were introduced for surgeons in 1889, were worn primarily to protect the surgeon's hands from the carbolic acid used to disinfect the instruments and not to stop him from infecting the patients!

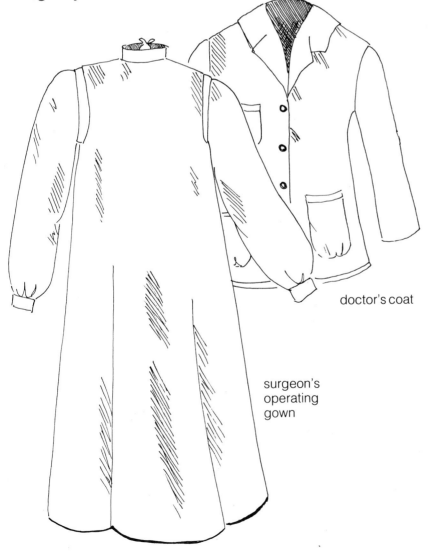

doctor's coat

surgeon's operating gown

A Young Housemaid, c. 1905

Dr and Mrs Westlake have only one maid. Her name is Alice. She is 15 and is the eldest daughter of a shepherd who works on the land owned by Lord Dudley. Here you can see Alice 'tramping the washing'. This custom originated in Scotland and was first described in 1635. In an age before washing machines, it was a way of getting the clothes clean – and keeping fit at the same time!

Alice is wearing a cotton print blouse, a white apron and a linen skirt. Obviously, she does not have the money to buy many clothes, so she often repairs her skirts and dresses when they become damaged or worn. Compare her clothing with that of Elizabeth, Lord Dudley's daughter, who is the same age. You might like to compare their very different lifestyles also.

On the right you can see Alice's father, Tom. He has come to the doctor's house to pay Dr Westlake for treating his daughter Jenny when she had whooping cough, an illness from which many children died at this time. It is not easy for Tom to find the money, but the doctor has agreed to accept payment in small instalments.

A Shepherd, c. 1905

Tom is wearing a corduroy coat and waistcoat, drill trousers, leather gaiters, stout boots and a felt hat. Gaiters, or leggings, were considered to be essential by country workers at this time. They helped to protect the trousers from mud and dirt, but they also kept the top of the boots tightly in at the ankle, which could be advantageous. In *Under the Greenwood Tree*, Thomas Hardy wrote that, when it was snowing, those villagers who were not wearing leggings, 'went into the stable and wound wisps of hay round their ankles to keep the insidious flakes from the interior of their boot'. If you look at paintings of country folk in Victorian or Edwardian days, you will notice that most of the men are wearing this kind of protection for their legs.

People like Tom were more concerned with the practicalities of clothing than with fashion.

The Shepherd's Family, c. 1905

Here is Tom's Family. His wife, Sarah, is in their cottage, busy at her spinning wheel, and she has her youngest child, little Tom, with her.

She is wearing a close-fitting lace cap, a knitted jerkin over a cotton shirt, a linen skirt and a cotton apron. Sarah tries to make as many clothes as she can in order to save money. She is good at knitting and sewing, and occasionally she makes garments for children in the village to earn a little extra money. Little Tom is wearing a loose cotton dress, once his sister's, over a flannel petticoat. He is playing with some unspun wool.

Jenny and Harry are playing outside. Harry is wearing a woollen hat and jumper and linen breeches. Jenny has on a white apron over a coarse linen dress, and she wears thick stockings and boots and a straw boater. You will notice that the boys are barefoot, even though it must be cold in the cottage.

Harry is playing with a toy
that he has made himself
from old wire, string and a
bent wheel. This is very
different to the smart
rocking horse in the
nursery at the
mansion. Try to find
out more about
children's toys in
Edwardian days
and draw pictures
of them. Perhaps you
could try to make some of them
yourself.

A Gypsy Family, c. 1906

A short distance from Tom's cottage there is a large field where a family of gypsies are encamped. Here you can see Sam and his wife, Meg, sitting outside their tent, which is made of tarpaulin and sacking. The caravan is in the background.

Sam is wearing a cloth cap, an old coat with an unmatching waistcoat, and checked woollen trousers. He has a cravat around his neck. Meg has on an unmatching cotten bodice and skirt and has a floral print scarf around her neck. Her felt hat is on the ground beside her.

Two of their daughters are pictured here. They are both wearing plain linen dresses which they have had for some time, darning and patching them when necessary. Kate has baby Joe on her knee. He is wearing a cotton print dress and a white smock. Meg made Joe's dress herself, and with some of the left-over material she made several scarves for herself and her daughters. The two girls only possess one dress each, so when they need to be cleaned they wash them in the river and wear only their petticoats whilst they are waiting for them to dry.

Meg and the girls often go out selling trinkets to earn money. Sam and Meg make wooden clothes pegs, and the girls help their mother by making and selling neckerchiefs and small bunches of herbs and flowers collected from the hedgerows.

Sometimes Meg needs to call in Dr Westlake. When she does she tries to persuade him to take a rabbit that Sam has caught whilst out poaching instead of his normal doctor's fee.

The Gypsy Children, c. 1906

Here are two more of Sam's children, Ned and Beccy. Ned is eight and is, therefore, old enough to be wearing trousers, but instead he has on one of his sister's old linen dresses, with a shabby knitted jumper over the top. Ned does not mind this because he has never known any different.

Beccy is collecting firewood. She is wearing a loose linen dress which has been bleached by the sun and is now a dull grey colour. On her feet she has a pair of very old boots which she has grown out of long ago.

Ned and Beccy do not go to school, even though the Education Act of 1870 made schooling compulsory for children between the ages of five and twelve. In fact, none of Sam's family can read or write apart from Meg, who can read a little and write her name. Sam does not think literacy necessary, for his family live by the laws of nature and have no need of books.

In Edwardian days the law was not very tolerant towards gypsies and they were often ordered to move on by the police. However, the roads were quiet and the countryside was peaceful, so they could quite easily find somewhere else to set up camp. Sam and his family value their freedom and would never exchange their travelling life for a more conventional home in a fixed place.

Can you imagine what it would be like to be a gypsy at the turn of the century? Do you think Alex or Amy would like to exchange their lifestyle for one as free as Ned and Beccy's? You could write a story about what happens when Alex and Amy swap lives with Ned and Beccy for a day.

A Garden Party, c. 1907

It is now the summer of 1907 and Lord Dudley is holding a garden party, followed by a ball in the evening. The ball is in Elizabeth's honour, to mark the occasion of her 'coming out'. This means that she has now made the transition from adolescence to womanhood and, henceforth, will be able to attend parties and do the London Season.

Here you can see some of the guests enjoying afternoon tea on the lawn. The ladies are wearing light summer dresses of satin and muslin, beautifully decorated with frills and lace. Their hats are trimmed with flowers, ribbons and feathers, and the lady on the right has a satin parasol resting against her chair.

You will notice that the men's costume is quite plain by comparison. They are dressed in silk top hats, morning coats and light trousers, and each is wearing a rose in his buttonhole.

Men's Evening Wear, c. 1907

It is now the evening and here we can see Lord Dudley at the grand ball. He is waiting for his wife and daughter Elizabeth to join him.

Lord Dudley is wearing a black tail coat and trousers, with a white waistcoat and tie and, on his feet, low pumps with bows on the front. Evening dress for men was a very formal affair at this time, and all the men at the ball would be dressed almost identically to Lord Dudley. You can imagine, therefore, that their dark, sombre outfits would make all the ladies' dresses seem all the more extravagant by comparison.

This social event is a very grand affair and has cost Lord Dudley a great deal of money. He has hired a band for the evening and there will be dancing as well as feasting. Try to find out more about the kind of dances that were popular at the turn of the century. A few years later the tango swept through Europe and people were enthusiastically dancing it wherever and whenever possible. (You can see an example of the kind of clothes they wore for this in the colour section.)

Compare the luxurious and extravagant lifestyle of Lord Dudley and his family with that of either Tom or Sam and their families.

Laundry girls, c. 1909

Chiffon day dress, c. 1907

In the garden, c. 1909

Dress for a garden party, c. 1913

Afternoon dress, c. 1913

Dress for the races, c. 1913

A Lady in pink, c. 1914

The tango, c. 1914

Two army privates, 1916-18

Women delivering coke during the war years

Rich and poor children, 1915-16

Ladies' Evening Wear, c. 1907

Here are Elizabeth and her mother arriving at the ball. They are both wearing beautiful silk dresses and evening gloves and have their hair swept up. The dresses are extravagantly trimmed with ribbon and lace, so you can imagine how expensive they must have been!

A Debutante, c. 1910

In Edwardian days, one important feature of the education of a young lady like Elizabeth would be the weekend parties that she would attend at large country houses. During these weekends away from home she would acquire many of the social skills and graces required of her. For a young girl, however, these parties could be quite an ordeal until she became more confident and self-assured.

It is now 1910 and Elizabeth is preparing to go away on a weekend visit. She takes with her a large trunk full of clothes because she will need many changes of dress. For example, a typical day might require the following: a riding or shooting outfit in the morning, a light dress for lunch, a tweed costume for an afternoon walk, a dress for tea and, finally, an evening outfit for dinner! One never wore the same outfit twice for dinner, and, of course, all these clothes required matching accessories, like those pictured here.

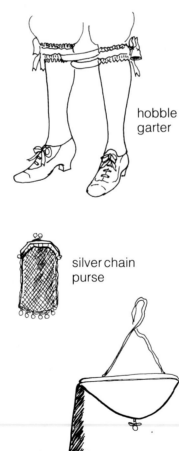

hobble garter

silver chain purse

evening bag, gloves and lace scarf

large handbag

34

In addition to all this, a young lady would require a large bag to carry around the house with her. This would contain her embroidery and perhaps a novel, in case she had any idle moments!

On the opposite page you can see Elizabeth in her travelling outfit, which is a tailored costume of white cloth decorated with large buttons. The skirt is very narrow and is called a hobble skirt. Elizabeth is wearing a hobble garter underneath this garment in order to prevent her from taking long strides which would split the material!

It was the fashion at this time for ladies' hips to appear very narrow, and this was accentuated by the large hats and huge handbags that were in vogue. Some of these handbags could be up to 30cm square!

One important item in Elizabeth's trunk is her tea gown. This was a popular garment in Edwardian days. It originated in the boudoir and was a loose, flowing dress with easy lines; it was usually decorated with an abundance of lace and trimmings. It was the custom to wear it at tea time and the sight of a lady floating along in her flimsy, uncorsetted gown was supposed to be real tonic for the men returning after a tiring round of golf or an afternoon's riding!

Elizabeth is wearing hers here. It is made of rose pink soft satin and is decorated with lace. It must have been a welcome change to wear something loose and flowing like this after being burdened with corsets all day long.

At The Theatre, c. 1910

It is now later in the year and Elizabeth is staying in London for a few days with her cousin Lydia. Here you can see them in a box at the theatre. As they are wealthy young ladies they are sitting in a box rather than in circle seats.

Elizabeth is on the left and she is wearing a theatre dress which is made of tulle lace over a taffeta base. It is decorated with velvet ribbon. Her hat is made of felt and has bird-of-paradise trimming.

Lydia's dress is also made of tulle lace. It is decorated with velvet ribbon and a matching belt with a gold clasp.

Both girls wear evening gloves and have opera glasses.

They are being escorted by Lydia's brother Robert, who is dressed in evening wear very similar to that worn by Lord Dudley at the ball three years before. Men's fashions were changing very little at this time and for a formal occasion such as this a dark suit and silk top hat would be considered correct. Robert is carrying his gloves and a waterproof coat.

In Edwardian times the London theatres were very interesting places to visit. There were many new plays to see by writers like James Barrie, Somerset Maugham and George Bernard Shaw. At the Savoy Theatre Gilbert and Sullivan operas were drawing many crowds and at Covent Garden opera-goers were hearing the music of Wagner, Verdi and Puccini for the first time. The music-halls were also popular, with their gay and sentimental songs and Cockney jokes, although these would be rather rough-and-ready places for young ladies like Elizabeth and Lydia.

Elizabeth and Lydia will probably see several plays and perhaps an opera during Elizabeth's stay in London. Find out more about popular music and theatre at this time. Which plays do you think Elizabeth and Lydia might have attended?

The Russian Ballet, c. 1911

Among the most exciting performances in London at this time were those of the Russian ballet. Anna Pavlova arrived in London in 1910 and soon became famous. Then, in 1911, Serge Diaghilev arrived with his company of dancers and his designer, Leon Bakst. The company took London by storm and Leon Bakst's costume designs, with their oriental flavour and fantastic colours, had an interesting effect on the world of fashion. Famous fashion designers like Paul Poiret and Lucille (Lady Duff-Gordon) were inspired by Bakst and began to incorporate an oriental look into their own fashion drawings.

Here is Nijinsky, a famous Russian dancer, and opposite are some fashion designs from 1912-13. You can see the similarities in style.

The result of this was that a wave of orientalism swept the fashion scene. Colours became more striking and soft drapery was preferred to rigid bodices and bell-shaped skirts.

Some rich ladies who really liked the romantic 'oriental' theme even took to wearing turbans and harem trousers which were visible beneath the hem of their skirts. These caused a sensation, however, and were only worn by the most daring!

Fashion Designs, c. 1912-13

1912

1913

1913

You might like to find out more about the Russian ballet and its influence on fashion, or you could look at the life and work of Paul Poiret, who was one of the most outstanding and unconventional designers of the time.

Street-Sellers, c. 1910

When Robert, Elizabeth and Lydia leave the warmth and gaiety of the theatre, they might very well meet people like Albert and Nell, pictured here. They are street-sellers. Albert is selling matches and collar studs and his wife is selling flowers.

Albert has tried to dress up for his work but his clothes are rather old and a little shabby. He is wearing a flat cap, a suit of wool and an old overcoat. Albert has had to resort to street-selling because he has been made redundant from his job as a weaver in a factory. He is now too old to find more work but too young to claim the old age pension which Lloyd George introduced in 1909. To claim this, he would have to be over 70.

Nell is wearing a straw bonnet decorated with flowers, and a woollen shawl over a plain linen dress. She is cold and tired, but the threatre-goers are usually generous, so she always accompanies Albert when he goes out at night.

It was women like Nell who inspired George Bernard Shaw to write his play *Pygmalion* in 1914, which later became the famous musical *My Fair Lady*. Try to find a copy of this play and read about the main character, Eliza Doolittle, who was a flower-seller like Nell.

A Salvation Army Shelter, c. 1910

Further away, in London's East End, near to where Nell and Albert live, these men are waiting for 'lights-out' in a Salvation Army shelter. They are homeless, and without this shelter they would be forced to spend the night on the streets. They possess only the clothes they are wearing and they will keep them on all night for warmth. The man second from the left is trying to repair his jacket. When he has done so he will put it back on to sleep in.

Have a look at the clothes of these men and think about their lifestyles. See if you can find out more about the very poor in the cities. How do you think their lives would compare with those of gypsy Sam and his family?

A Shopkeeper and His Family, c. 1910

This is Albert's younger brother, Joseph, who owns a small and successful grocery store in London. He is pictured here with his wife, Winifred, who often helps him in the shop and with the accounts.

Winifred is wearing a high-necked frilly blouse with three-quarter length sleeves, and a dark grey skirt of serge. This outfit is smart, but at the same time it is practical for her work. You would not see Winifred in ornate dresses like Lady Constance or Elizabeth because they would be beyond her financial means and also out of place in the grocery shop.

Joseph is wearing a lounge suit, a white shirt with a bow tie, and leather shoes. He has his watch in his waistcoat pocket. Albert is very proud of this watch as it was once his father's. He intends to give it to his eldest son, Fred, when he is 21.

Here are Joseph's eldest sons, Fred, who is 15, and Jack, who is 12. They are busy in the shop, wrapping up groceries into brown paper parcels for their customers.

Fred and Jack are both in their shirt sleeves, but they are wearing smart, single-breasted waistcoats with matching trousers, and they also have collars and ties. Fred is wearing a white apron to protect his clothes when he is measuring out flour.

Compare this kind of small, family-run, shop with the large supermarket chains that we have today. What are the advantages and disadvantages of each?

At the Races, c. 1914

It is now 1914, and Lady Dudley and Elizabeth are at a race meeting. They are accompanied by Julian, Elizabeth's fiancé, who is a friend of her cousin Robert's.

You can see that the fashionable look for ladies is a long, narrow one. Lady Dudley is wearing a short jacket trimmed with feathers. It has three-quarter length sleeves. Her lightweight dress has a hobble skirt and a three-quarter length overskirt. She is wearing a wide-brimmed hat and carries a parasol.

Elizabeth is dressed in a high-waisted, V-necked summer dress of white wool. The wrap-around skirt is held with elastic at the waist, and the long-sleeved bodice is made of lace. Over this she is wearing a jacket with short, kimono sleeves, fastened with a cord in front. Her short white gloves are made of leather and her feathered hat is decorated with an osprey plume. She is holding a long-handled, lace-covered parasol, and her handbag, which has a metal frame and fringe trimming.

Looking at the dresses of these two women, you can see how much the shape of fashion has altered since the beginning of the century. The stiff, rigid petticoats are gone, along with the bell-shaped skirts, and the whole appearance is much softer. However, the ladies are just as restricted, not by masses of petticoats, but by their hobble skirts and garters!

Julian is wearing a single-breasted lounge suit with small-checked trousers and a waistcoat, a bow-tie, white gloves and spats, and a silk top hat.

None of these spectators is watching the races, however, as their attention has been drawn to something which is happening among the crowds. . .

The Suffragettes, c. 1914

Some yards away, there is quite a commotion. A young Suffragette, who has been taking part in a loud and noisy demonstration, is being forcibly removed from the race meeting by two of the stewards. Lady Dudley is horrified to see that the Suffragette is her niece Lydia, who has recently joined the Women's Social and Political Union and has been vigorously campaigning for women's rights.

Lydia, her friend Marcia, and several other women have been selling posters and papers advertising their campaign, but some of them have been arrested for being too noisy and aggressive.

Both girls are wearing practical, tailor-made outfits of light wool, wide-brimmed straw hats, and gloves. It is interesting that the Suffragettes were campaigning for freedom and equality at the very time that fashion was dictating that they should be bound and fettered by hobble skirts, which could not be more restricting. You will notice that Lydia, Marcia and the girl depicted in the poster, who all represent freedom, are wearing more practical outfits than Lady Dudley and Elizabeth.

The two stewards are both wearing woollen lounge suits with turn-up trousers, straw boaters and striped ties.

They are particularly anxious to control any disturbance at the race meeting as they do not want a repetition of the incident on Derby Day 1913, when another Suffragette, Emily Davison, threw herself under the King's horse and died for her cause.

Try to find out more about the Suffragette movement and look at the life of one of its most famous leaders, Mrs Emmeline Pankhurst.

In Prison, c. 1914

Lydia has been arrested, tried and sent to prison for three months.

Before being admitted to prison she had to submit to a compulsory bath and medical examination. She then had her personal belongings confiscated and was given a prison uniform of coarse serge, which you can see her wearing here. It is very unbecoming and quite different to the fine, fancy dresses she used to wear. The rest of her prison outfit consists of a white linen cap and a checked apron. She has a tea-towel at her waist, ready for her work in the prison kitchen.

Some of the other women prisoners are already working in the kitchens. They are being watched by a rather stern-faced prison warder, who is dressed in a black linen dress and cap and has a chatelaine suspended from her waist.

Lydia's cell is 4 metres long by 2 metres wide, and her bed consists of a plank with a mattress and two blankets. Her meals are mostly starch. For breakfast she has bread; for dinner, an oatmeal gruel known as 'stirabout'; and for supper, bread again. Some of the Suffragettes used to go on hunger strike and were often force-fed by the prison authorities. This treatment, in fact, helped to further the prisoners' cause because it gained them public sympathy.

49

Two Soldiers, c. 1915

It is now 1915 and England is in the grip of war. At first, when the war began in August 1914, everyone expected that it would be over by Christmas, but as the months dragged on it became clear that it was to be a long drawn-out affair and that it would alter the lives of many many people.

Many of the young men you have met in this book are now in the army. Alfred and William, Lord Dudley's two elder sons, and Julian, Elizabeth's fiancé, have received their commission. Fred, the grocer's son, and Harry, the shepherd's eldest boy, have both joined up as soldiers. It is quite possible that they will all fight in the same battles and that they will be comrades together, even though they come from such different backgrounds.

Alfred is on the station platform, waiting to begin his long journey to the front. He is wearing his khaki uniform and carrying his coat and equipment. One item of interest is his bandolier, a shoulder belt with pouches in which he carries his cartridges. The long strips of cloth wound around his leg from the ankle to the knee are known as puttees and give him protection and support.

Alfred has his steel helmet over his shoulder and a haversack on his back in which he is carrying items such as dry socks, a towel and his washing and eating kit.

At the same time, Fred is saying goodbye to his mother in London. He, too, is carrying a lot of equipment on his back. You can see his water bottle, his tin mug and his haversack. Can you find out what might be contained in the other bags on his back? How heavy do you think all this equipment would be?

Fred's mother is wearing a linen smock over her blouse and skirt, as she has been helping her son to pack and did not wish to damage her clothes.

She is very proud of Fred, but, at the same time, is afraid for his safety. Can you imagine how it would feel to be in these circumstances?

The Women's Police Service, c. 1916

With so many men away fighting in the war, there were not enough trained people to cover all the work that needed to be done at home, so people began to do jobs that they had not been trained for. Three million of this new workforce were women.

In April 1915 Mrs Pankhurst had called on her Suffragettes to abandon their fight against the government and, instead, to join in the war effort and fight for their country against the common enemy. Now, women who had been active in the Suffragette movement worked hard in all kinds of important jobs. In this way they not only helped in the war effort but also proved that they were equal to men.

Here are Lydia and Marcia who have joined the Women's Police Service. Their uniform consists of a Norfolk jacket in 'police blue', bearing the letters W.P.V. on the shoulder straps. Their skirts are reasonably full, allowing for them to give chase if necessary.

The round hats, worn by the rank and file, are modified ladies' riding hats. This is because the lady who designed the uniform, Margaret Damer Dawson, felt that riding hats might 'withstand the weather and a sharp blow on the head if necessary'.

Lydia and Marcia do not carry any weapons and their work mainly involves community service, such as safeguarding women travellers and supervising children in the streets.

The Women's Auxiliary Army Corps, c. 1916

The Women's Auxiliary Army Corps was formed in 1916 and attracted 50,000 women in the first few months. Here is Anne, the doctor's daughter, who has joined the W.A.A.C. Her smart khaki uniform consists of a hip-length, belted tunic and calf-length skirt, and she has her wide-brimmed felt hat turned up at the side, rather like the Australian troops.

Women like Anne often served in France as cooks in the army camps. This was quite an experience for the soldiers, who were unused to being supervised by women. Those women working in Britain were allowed to do so from home, and because of this it was felt that recruits should be drawn only from the middle and upper middle classes. This was because it was feared that the poorer women might steal the army food and take it home for their families. In fact, a large number of poor women did try to join the W.A.A.C. So many of them were riddled with lice and had an inadequate supply of underclothing that the Chief Controller issued a list of articles that were essential before any woman could be drafted into a unit. The list was as follows:

'1 pair of strong shoes or boots (in addition to the free issue)
1 pair low-heeled shoes for housewear
2 pairs khaki stockings (in addition to the free issue)
2 pairs at least warm combinations
2 pairs dark coloured knickers with washable linings
2 warm vests of loosely woven shetland wool
1 doz khaki handkerchiefs
2 pairs pyjamas or 2 strong nightdresses
burning sanitary towels

It is advisable if possible to bring as well a jersey or golf jacket which should be worn under the frock coat in cold weather.'

The W.A.A.C. was organized in four sections: Cookery, Mechanical, Clerical and Miscellaneous.

Do you think it was fair that poorer women were not welcome in the W.A.A.C.? Why do you think they wished to join?

A Munitions Factory, c. 1916

New factories were opened in order to increase the production of arms and ammunition, and these also employed thousands of women. Young girls like Ellen and Susan, for example, who had been working as domestic servants for about £2 per month, jumped at the chance of a job in a factory where they could earn £5 a week. The work was hard and sometimes dangerous, but the girls enjoyed the new-found independence which came with their weekly wages.

Here is Ellen, seen operating a rifling machine in a gun factory. She is wearing a thick cotton overall, baggy cotton trousers and a mob cap. It is important that her hair is covered so that it does not catch in the machinery.

Ellen's work is heavy and she is often much too hot in all her protective clothing. She is thinking of having her hair cut short, as many of her friends have done, as this would be cooler and more convenient for her. It is a very different uniform to that which she left behind at Lord Dudley's.

Susan's work is more dangerous than Ellen's because it involves handling gunpowder shells. She has to wear special gloves and a mask so that her face does not turn yellow from the fumes.

Other girls like Ellen and Susan are working as window-cleaners, road-sweepers, stokers and even in the shipyards.

Try to find pictures of women working in these various jobs and draw the different costumes they are wearing.

The Women's Land Army, c. 1916

The Women's Land Army, for agricultural work at home, was formed at the same time as the W.A.A.C. It was divided into three sections: agricultural, timber-cutting and forage. A handbook was issued to all members and laid down the following rule regarding appearance and behaviour:

'You are doing a man's work and so you're dressed like a man, but remember just because you wear a smock and breeches you should take care to behave like a British girl, who expects chivalry and respect from everyone she meets.'

Here is Jenny, the shepherd's daughter. She is wearing knickerbockers and leggings under her overall and is out helping in the fields. Her thick gloves protect her hands whilst she is working with her scythe.

The war swept away social conventions and made drastic changes which affected everyone. Rich women lost their servants and found themselves doing the shopping and cleaning for the first time. Factory girls found a new independence with their bigger wage packets. Girls like Lydia and Marcia proved that women were capable of taking up responsible positions in professions previously reserved for men. This was, therefore, the true beginning of women's emancipation, although there was still a long way to go before Britain would see the first woman Prime Minister!

55

Voluntary Aid Detachments, c. 1916

The Voluntary Aid Detachments, (V.A.D.s), were founded by the Red Cross and the St John's Ambulance Brigade in 1910. During the war years many women, eager to help in the war effort, flocked to join these detachments to give their services as nurses in temporary hospitals around the country.

They wore the uniform of their particular detachment, blue for the Red Cross and grey for the St John's Ambulance Brigade, with a red cross or the St John emblem on their aprons.

Many of these women were young ladies like Elizabeth who had never had to do more for themselves than pour out cups of tea or put pins in their hair. Now, with the minimum of training, they were asked to cook, clean, lift, carry and dress horrific wounds.

Elizabeth is working for the Red Cross at a temporary hospital in Devon. She is wearing the Red Cross uniform with a handkerchief-style hat. There were two types of collar, both of which are pictured here. The Peter Pan style was soft and much more comfortable than the stiff white one, which tended to chafe the neck.

Elizabeth finds the work very demanding. Sometimes she slips out into the garden to read a letter from her fiancé or one of her brothers. She is very anxious for their safety now, as the war has already claimed millions of lives.

Try to find out more about the work of V.A.D.s. How do you think this change of lifestyle would affect girls like Elizabeth? Why do you think they volunteered? Vera Brittain was a young lady from a similar background to Elizabeth, who broke off her studies at Oxford to become a V.A.D. She wrote a book of her experiences called *Testament of Youth*, which you might like to look up in your local library. You could also find out about Edith Cavell, another famous British nurse who served in the First World War.

The War Drags On . . . c. 1917

The war also greatly affected the fashion scene. Materials were in short supply, and as so many women were doing manual work the demand was for more practical clothing. Dresses became shorter and had more simple lines. By 1917 skirts had risen to eight inches above the ground.

When Elizabeth is not at the hospital, she might wear a tailor-made costume such as the one pictured here. It is made of serge and has a 'military'-look jacket. She is also wearing laced boots and a small hat decorated with a velvet ribbon. You will notice, too, that she has had her hair cut short.

Meanwhile, in London, Winifred is reading a letter from her son, Fred. She is wearing a blouse of cotton voile, a plain navy skirt and stout shoes.

Winifred's clothes have not changed much during the war years. The grocery shop is not doing well because of the difficulty in getting supplies, so she does not have much money to spare. Also, she is too preoccupied with thoughts of her son to be bothered with the latest fashion.

Fred's letter makes her very sad. Any ideas of a soldier's life being glorious or heroic have long been forgotten. Instead, his letters tell of the appalling conditions in the trenches at the Western Front and the horrific sensation of continually sinking into the Flanders mud.

Here you can see Fred and some of his fellow soldiers. They have been issued with supplementary clothing to protect them from the cold and wet because their uniforms are so inadequate. Fred is wearing a leather sleeveless coat over his uniform, and the soldier behind him has on a sleeveless leather jerkin. They are both wearing rubber waders. These have been issued to all ranks because the foul, muddy conditions have caused many foot disorders, which were termed 'trench feet'. The bars on their left sleeves are their battalion identification.

Conclusion

In November 1918, just when it seemed as though the war would surely go on for ever, the fighting suddenly came to an end. People went wild with excitement and celebrations were held up and down the country.

Life could never be the same as it had been before the war, however, because so much had changed. It was as if the whole structure of society had been turned upside down. Many women had to surrender their well-paid jobs to men returning from the war but, even so, they had proved themselves equal to men, and women over 30 were now able to vote. Most important, perhaps, was the change in outlook of women themselves. They had tasted the independence and sense of freedom that had come with their factory jobs. Many of them had found that their children were better clothed and fed during the war than before it because, with the separation allowance they received while their husbands were away and their own earnings, they had been much better off. For the first time, thousands of women had experienced the joys of achievement. They were not likely to forget this and would fight even harder for equality in the future.

Fashions had altered, too. Skirts were shorter and allowed more freedom of movement, unlike the restricting hobble skirts women had been wearing at the beginning of the war. Many ladies now wore their hair in the popular short bob style which gave them a boyish look rather than emphasizing their femininity.

There had been a relaxing of the strict conventions that had governed men's wear, too. The silk hat had almost disappeared and the morning coat was worn only by people like politicians, doctors and stockbrokers. Most men adopted the lounge suit for everyday wear, or a tweed sports coat with flannel trousers.

evening
dress, c. 1918

60

Amy and Alex, two of Lord Dudley's children, are pictured here. Amy is now a young woman of 18 and is wearing an evening dress of crepe de chine and black satin. Alex is in a lounge suit made of wool. Turn back to the pictures of their parents in 1903 and compare the changes in dress that have taken place.

Finally, perhaps you would like to think about some of the young men who never returned home: Fred, the grocer's son, the shepherd's son Harry, Lord Dudley's son Alfred, and Julian, Elizabeth's fiancé. They were all young men from different backgrounds but, in uniform, they were all soldiers who died for the same cause. Do you think a uniform can sweep away the barriers of social class? You might like to consider this in relation to the women you have seen in uniform as well as the soldiers.

In the short space of a few years, a major social upheaval totally changed people's attitudes and opinions, and these changes, in turn, influenced the clothes they wore. In fashion, the movement was from the extravagant luxury of the beginning of the century towards a greater simplicity and freedom at the end of the war. Do you think these changes were for the better? Many people consider that the Edwardian years were the last 'golden' years for the upper classes. What is your opinion of this?

lounge
suit,
c. 1918

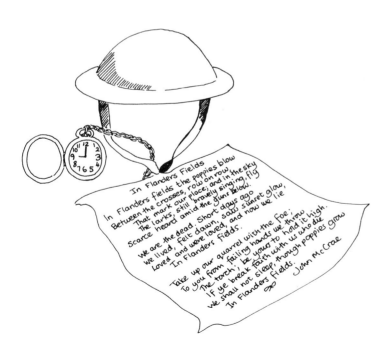

In Flanders Fields
In Flanders fields the poppies blow
Between the crosses, row on row,
That mark our place; and in the sky
The larks, still bravely singing, fly
Scarce heard amid the guns below.

We are the dead. Short days ago
We lived, felt dawn, saw sunset glow,
Loved and were loved, and now we lie
In Flanders fields.

Take up our quarrel with the foe:
To you from failing hands we throw
The torch; be yours to hold it high.
If ye break faith with us who die
We shall not sleep, though poppies grow
In Flanders fields. John McCrae

Glossary

bandolier	a shoulder belt used for carrying cartridges *(page 50)*
boudoir	a lady's small, private room *(page 35)*
breeches	short trousers, fastened below the knee *(pages 9 and 24)*
cashmere	a fine, soft wool *(page 8)*
chaperon	a married or elderly woman in charge of a girl on social occasions *(page 13)*
combinations	a one-piece woollen undergarment with long sleeves and legs *(page 53)*
debutante	a young girl being presented to society *(page 34)*
chatelaine	a set of chains suspended from the waist and used for carrying keys *(page 48)*
gaiters	a covering for the leg below the knee, usually made of tough cloth or leather *(pages 9, 14 and 23)*
galoshes	an overshoe of rubber to keep the shoes clean and dry *(page 11)*
hobble skirt	a very narrow skirt which prevented women from walking with anything more than short, shuffling steps *(pages 34, 44 and 45)*
holland	a linen fabric *(page 21)*
khaki	fabric of twilled cotton or wool *(pages 50 and 53)*
kimono	a long, loose Japanese robe with wide, short sleeves *(page 44)*
knickerbockers	loose-fitting breeches gathered at the knee *(page 55)*
leggings	outer covering of leather for the legs; *see* gaiters *(page 55)*
lounge suit	a matching jacket and trousers suit, the jacket having a short skirt with rounded corners at the front and being slightly fitted at the waist. *(pages 42, 47 and 61)*
puttees	long strips of cloth which are wound round the leg from the ankle to the knee for protection and support *(page 50)*
serge	a kind of durable, twilled, worsted fabric *(pages 20, 42 and 58)*
S-bend	the fashionable shape for ladies at the beginning of the century. It was achieved by wearing corsets which emphasized the bust and bottom and flattened the stomach *(pages 11 and 64)*
spats	short gaiters covering the instep and reaching a little above the ankle *(page 8)*
tea gown	a light, loose gown with an abundance of trimmings. Worn when relaxing *(page 35)*
tulle	fine silk net used for veils and dresses *(page 37)*
voile	a thin, semi-transparent cotton, woollen or silken dress material *(pages 12 and 58)*

c. 1913
– a special 'sports' corset
advertised in 1913 as
being suitable for
the Tango

Book List

Bingham, Stella	*Ministering Angels*, Osprey Publishing, 1979
Black, J.A. & Garland, M.	*A History of Fashion*, Orbis Publishing, 1975
Bradfield, Nancy	*Costume in Detail 1730-1930*, Harrap, 1968
Bradfield, Nancy	*Historical Costumes of England 1066-1956*, Harrap, 1958
Braun-Ronsdorf, Margarete	*The Wheel of Fashion 1789-1929*, Thames & Hudson, 1964
Carter, Ernestine	*Twentieth-Century Fashion*, Eyre Methuen, 1975
Cassin-Scott, Jack	*Costume and Fashion in Colour 1760-1920*, Blandford Press, 1980
Contini, Mila	*Fashion from Ancient Egypt to the Present Day*, Hamlyn, 1965
Cunnington, C.W. & P.	*History of Underclothes*, revised ed. Faber & Faber, 1981
Cunnington, P.	*The Costume of Household Servants*, A. & C. Black, 1974
Cunnington, P. & Lucas, C.	*Occupational Costume in England*, A. & C. Black, 1964
Cunnington, P. & Mansfield, A.	*Handbook of English Costume in the Twentieth Century*, Faber & Faber, 1973
Dunbar, John Telfer	*Herself – the Life and Photographs of M.E.M. Donaldson*, Blackwood, 1979
Fosten, D.S.V. & Marrion, R.J.	*The British Army 1914-18*, Osprey Publishing, 1978
Laver, James	*Costume through the Ages*, Thames & Hudson, 1964
Laver, James	*Edwardian Promenade*, Edward Hulton & Co, 1958
Marwick, Arthur	*Women at War 1914-18*, Fontana, 1977
	Pictorial Encyclopaedia of Fashion, Hamlyn, 1968
Priestly, J.B.,	*The Edwardians*, Heinemann, 1970
Raeburn, Antonia	*The Suffragette View*, David & Charles, 1976
Sichel, Marion	*Costume Reference, Volume 7: The Edwardians*, Batsford, 1978
Streatfield, Noel (ed.)	*The Day before Yesterday*, Collins, 1956
Stevenson, Pauline	*Edwardian Fashion*, Ian Allan, 1980
Trease, Geoffrey	*Living Through History: The Edwardian Era*, Batsford, 1986
Wilson, Eunice	*A History of Shoe Fashion*, Pitman, 1974
Winter, Gordon	*A Country Camera 1844-1914*, Penguin, 1960
Winter, Gordon	*The Golden Years 1903-1913*, Penguin, 1975

Places to Visit

Here are a few ideas for some interesting places to visit connected with costume in Edwardian days and during the First World War.

Bath Museum of Costume, Assembly Rooms, Bath, Avon.

Bethnal Green Museum of Childhood (a branch of the Victoria and Albert Museum).

Gallery of English Costume, Platt Hall, Platt Fields, Rusholme, Manchester M14 5LL.

Geffrye Museum, Kingsland Road, Shoreditch, London E2 8EA.

Imperial War Museum, Lambeth Road, London SE1 6HZ.

Museum of London, London Wall, London EC2Y 5HN.

National Army Museum, Royal Hospital Road, London SW3 4HT.

Victoria and Albert Museum, Cromwell Road, South Kensington, London SW7 2RL.

Things to Do

1. Ask your grandparents if they have any old photographs of your family in Edwardian times. What kind of clothes are they wearing?

2. Visit your local museum and find out if they have any examples of clothes from Edwardian days for you to look at. Ask also if they have any interesting items relating to the First World War.

3. The Wright Brothers flew in public for the first time in 1908. See if you can discover what kind of clothes were worn for flying. Draw some pictures of clothing worn in different types of sporting activities in Edwardian times.

4. Find a book on army uniforms and draw some of the soldiers from the different regiments. How suitable were the uniforms for life in the trenches? Try to find out more about the war poets – for example, Wilfred Owen and Rupert Brooke.

5. Find out all you can about the different jobs that women did during the war years. Look at the kind of clothes they wore for these jobs and compare them with the fashions that they had been wearing previously.

6. Find out more about the Russian ballet and its influence on fashion in the years immediately following its visit to Europe. Some of the costume designs were unusual and very colourful. Try designing some ballet costumes of your own.

7. Discover all you can about the manufacture of some of the beautiful dresses described at the beginning of the book. Look at the textiles used, the conditions in which the seamstresses worked and at some of the fashion designs of the time.

8. Try making a hobble garter, (p. 34). How do you think it would feel to wear one of these all day? Do you think women will ever wear this kind of restrictive clothing again?

9. Write to some of the large department stores in London – for example, Liberty & Co. or Harrods. Ask them if they can let you have any information on the type of clothes that they sold in Edwardian times. Compare these clothes and the cost of them with similar items today.